THINGS YOU SHOULD KNOW ABOUT

OWLS

By Steve Parker
Illustrated by Andrea Morandi

BARDFIELD
PRESS

First published by Bardfield Press in 2006
Copyright © Miles Kelly Publishing Ltd 2006

Bardfield Press is an imprint of
Miles Kelly Publishing Ltd
Bardfield Centre
Great Bardfield
Essex, CM7 4SL

2 4 6 8 10 9 7 5 3 1

Editorial Director: Belinda Gallagher
Art Director: Jo Brewer
Designer: HERRINGBONE Design
Production: Elizabeth Brunwin
Reprographics: Mike Coupe, Stephan Davis
Indexer: Jane Parker

ISBN 1-84236-751-X

Printed in China

www.mileskelly.net
info@mileskelly.net

British Library Cataloguing-in-Publication Data.
A catalogue record for this book is available
from the British Library

Contents

Barn owls live nearly everywhere

BARN OWLS do not just live in barns. They rest and nest in church towers, old buildings, hollow trees and caves in cliffs. Also they live in many different places, from cold mountains to tropical forests.

The barn owl is one of the most widespread birds. It is found in the far north, the far south – and everywhere between!

Owl facts

• The barn owl is about 35 centimetres long, from beak to tail-tip.

• It lays more eggs than any other owl – in some years there can be more than ten.

Too bright

Barn owls swoop on animals injured by cars on roads – then get blinded by headlights and cannot see to fly away.

Barn owls catch a huge range of prey, from mice, rats and voles, to baby birds, lizards, grubs, beetles and worms.

The barn owl is snow-white underneath, and looks ghostly in the moonlight.

The owl swoops out of the darkness in deathly silence. It holds its wings still, and its soft-edged feathers make no sound.

The barn owl's feet have strong toes and long claws called talons. These jab into the prey and hold it with a powerful grip.

Owls fly by day!

Owl facts
• The snowy is one of the largest owls, measuring up to 70 centimetres from beak to tail-tip.
• It is the biggest hunting bird of the Arctic region.

Most owls fly secretly at night. But the **SNOWY OWL** of the far north flies in daylight too. It has no choice. During the short summer, its Arctic home is the 'land of the midnight sun'. There is no darkness at all!

The snowy owl cannot nest in trees as there are none on the rocky, grassy northern lands called the Arctic tundra.

6

A hunting owl flies slowly and silently, wing-tip feathers spread and body swaying. Its head is held steady, looking and listening for prey.

Snowy owls nest in a hollow among stones and moss. The female lays up to ten eggs over three to four weeks. If prey is scarce, she lays just one. She tears up the meaty meals for her chicks.

Snowy owls catch lemmings, mice, voles, rats, rabbits, and many kinds of small birds. The male brings food to the nest.

Whoo's whoo?

In most owls, female and male look similar. The male snowy has fewer dark flecks than the female – he is almost pure white.

Owls go fishing

Many owls hunt over land. **FISH OWLS** fly over rivers and lakes in the moonlight. They look and listen for ripples and bubbles, which are signs of fish or similar creatures just under the water. To catch their prey, fish owls do not mind getting their feet wet!

Owl facts

• There are seven kinds of fish owl across Africa, South Asia and East Asia.

• Blakiston's fish owl of China and Japan is huge, with wings nearly 2 metres across.

Wading in water

Owls do not always swoop from the air. The fish owl may go paddling in shallow water, using its feet to help it find food.

Fish owls have legs, toes and claws that are all extra-long. Their legs are mostly bare, because feathers would get wet and heavy.

Fish owls eat more than fish. They grab lizards, frogs, freshwater crabs and crayfish, small waterbirds, water-rats and water-voles. They even take young rabbits that come to the water's edge for a drink.

The fish owl skims over the surface, aiming towards the bubbles and ripples. It then flicks out its long legs to grab its slippery supper from just under the water.

The owl's toes are covered with tiny scales. They help its long, sharp talons (claws) to grip the smooth, scaly, wriggly fish.

Owls go to church

Owl facts

- The little owl is not the smallest owl, but it is little – about 20 centimetres from beak to tail-tip.
- It lives across the whole of Asia, from Spain to China, and also in North Africa.

LITTLE OWLS also go to temples, shrines and mosques. They like the tall towers and quiet surroundings. By day they roost (rest) and at night they hunt in parks, gardens and fields.

Little owls often come out just before dusk. They are more likely to be seen by people than owls that fly at night.

Small and short

The well-named little owl is quite a bit smaller than a pigeon, or even a blackbird, although like most owls, its tail is short.

Since ancient times, little owls have lived in towns and cities. Swooping from a church or temple, they were seen as symbols of wisdom and good luck.

The little owl's loud calls carry a long way in the still of the evening. They include 'kee-uuw', like a loud cat's miaow, and 'wheere-ooww', similar to a dog's yelp.

In the countryside, little owls prefer old trees such as oaks, willows and palms. They like the holes that form where branches have broken.

Little owls hunt little prey – worms, beetles, slugs and spiders. A mouse or sparrow is a huge feast for the little owl!

Owls have no horns!

Owl facts

• The great horned owl is widespread in North and South America, in forests, woods, parks, scrub and desert.

• It is about 50 centimetres from beak to tail-tip.

The **GREAT HORNED OWL** has tufts of feathers on its head. They look like horns, or ears. But an owl's real ears are hidden by its plumage (feathers). An owl can hear as well as it can see — or even better!

The ears of the great horned owl are on the sides of its head, at about the same • • • • • • • • • level as the eyes.

What big eyes!

Make an owl head as big as a human one, with a face mask from card. See how huge the eyes are — bigger than yours!

12

The deep hooting of the male means: 'Other owls stay away.' He makes four deep hoots, 'boo-whoo-whoo-whoo'.

At breeding time, a nearby female great horned owl answers back. She makes about seven hoots that are even deeper!

Then the two get together and make yet more strange noises which sound like cats purring, babies crying and people laughing.

The owl's powerful hooked bill (beak) tears up mice, rats, rabbits, gophers, prairie dogs, and even squirrels and small monkeys.

Some owls have lots of names

Owl facts
- The boobook owl lives in Southeast Asia, south-eastern Australia and New Zealand.
- Its many noises include a squeal like cats fighting.

The **BOOBOOK OWL** is named after its 'booo-book' call. It is also called the morepork or mopoke owl, after its other calls. And the cat owl, too — it can miaow!

Boobook owls are common in some areas, and do not mind living around villages and towns. In early evening they even perch in the open, on a street light or telephone pole — or on a branch in a garden.

Boobooks eat mainly insects, such as cockchafer beetles and moths, which swarm around street lights. They also catch small birds, mice and baby rats.

The male and female owls call softly to each other as they get ready for the night's hunting. When they have chicks, they need to find food by day as well.

Mobbed!

If small birds find a resting owl, they 'mob' it by flapping and squawking to drive it away. After all, when darkness falls, it might eat them!

Many owls are tawny

Owl facts
- The tawny owl lives in all kinds of woodlands and forests across Europe and Asia.
- It is about 40 centimetres long from beak to tail-tip.

Tawny is a colour – a sort of orange-reddish brown. Many owls are tawny, but only one is called the **TAWNY OWL**. In the breeding season, the male calls as he returns with food for the female and chicks.

Tawny owls like plenty of trees but they can also live in towns and farmland. A female and male stay together for many years. They raise their family in the same area, or territory, year after year.

16

Too fluffy to fly

Owl chicks have soft, fluffy feathers to keep them warm. They grow stronger feathers when they are ready to fly.

Tawny owls like to nest in a tree hole. But they might also use a hollow among the roots, or even the old nest of a magpie or squirrel.

There are usually three eggs, which hatch after four weeks. The chicks are ready to fly off on their own when they are about five weeks old.

Owls can screech!

Which night creatures screech loudly? **SCOPS OWLS** do, time after time, calling 'chiup' every few seconds, on and on, and on and on. They keep people awake at night! This is why they are also known as screech-owls. Even though they make so much noise, they are very difficult to see!

Owls roost (sleep) during the day. But their feathers blend so well into the background of tree trunks, branches and twigs, it is almost impossible to spot them. Merging with the background like this is called camouflage.

When a Scops owl is out in the open, it stays perfectly still, so it is hardly noticed. It watches for danger through narrowed eye-slits.

Owl pellets

An owl cannot digest hard bones, claws and beaks in its food. So it coughs up these bits, all pressed together into a lump called a pellet.

Like other 'eared' owls, the tufts on top of the Scops owl's head are not real ears, but long feathers.

Like most birds, an owl moults – grows new feathers as the old ones fall out, usually twice each year. Moulting is a risky time because the owl cannot fly well until its new plumage is complete.

Owls like spikes

Owl facts
• Sometimes the elf owl owl flies near campfires of people, chasing insects attracted by the light.
• It is about 14 centimetres from beak to tail-tip.

The **ELF OWL** is one of the tiniest owls. It could easily sit in your hand (if it was tame). But even though it is so small, it has little to fear when at home. Its nest hole is in a tree-sized cactus called the giant saguaro. It is one of the prickliest places in the world.

The giant saguaro is a very tall plant. The elf owl's nest hole might be 10 metres above the ground. •••••••••••

Fierce food!

An owl's meals often fight back when caught! Worms wriggle, beetles and crickets kick and spiders bite.

The elf owl is usually too small to hunt mice. Its main meals are moths, grubs, caterpillars, crickets, beetles, centipedes, spiders and worms. It grabs many of these from the ground.

The female elf owl lays about three tiny eggs, hardly larger than grapes.

Both female and male incubate the eggs (sit on them to keep them warm) for two weeks until they hatch.

In their homeland of southwestern North America, elf owls do not just live in cactus deserts. They are also found in bushy areas and woods, especially along steep valleys and cliffs.

Owls kill owls!

Owl facts
• The eagle owl is probably the biggest owl, about 70 centimetres from beak to tail-tip.
• It is found across most of Europe, North Africa and Asia – but it is getting more scarce.

The **EAGLE OWL** is so big and strong that it hunts other hunters. It may catch another owl, like a tawny, or a bird of prey like a buzzard or goshawk, sleeping on a branch.

Eagle versus owl
An eagle owl can weigh as much as an eagle, although it has a bigger head and shorter tail.

Eagle owls can hunt large prey and have been known to attack small deer and even foxes.

The eagle owl is found mainly in high mountains and rocky, dry scrubland. Even real eagles keep away from this powerful predator.

Ear tufts on the eagle owl's head have nothing to do with its hearing. It is thought they may help to camouflage (hide) the owl in its surroundings.

The eagle owl's massive claws stab into its prey like curved nails. There is no escape for the victim.

Woodland is being cut down where these owls like to nest. The eagle owl is becoming scarce because of this.

Index